Not long ago, Craig Claiborne, the world's most renowned food writer and chef, was told to change his eating habits—or else. His blood pressure was soaring, his doctor said, and he was on the verge of a stroke.

Unwilling to compromise his love of culinary excellence, Claiborne developed a low-sodium diet that stabilized his blood pressure and allowed him to lose 25 pounds—while continuing to enjoy everything from bread and pasta to meats and sauces and even exquisite desserts.

Now he shares what is surely the greatest boon of all time to good eating *and* good health.

CRAIG CLAIBORNE'S GOURMET DIET